THE
COWGIRL'S
GUIDE TO LIFE

THE QUOTATIONS IN THIS BOOK COME FROM A MIXTURE OF LORE AND EXPERIENCE.

THE
COWGIRL'S
GUIDE TO LIFE

Gladiola Montana and Texas Bix Bender

THE CODE OF HER WEST:

USE A SHORT ROPE,
A SWEET SMILE,
AND A HOT BRAND.

THERE'S NO CURE FOR LOVE SICKNESS, AND NOBODY REALLY WANTS ONE.

THERE ARE TWO THINGS A MAN
MUST DO TO KEEP HIS WIFE HAPPY.
FIRST, LET HER THINK SHE'S
GETTING HER WAY.
SECOND, LET HER HAVE IT.

ONE OF THESE DAYS IS NONE OF THESE DAYS.

Sometimes flowers don't
say it very well.

You need to explain yourself.

Be sure to taste your words
before you spit 'em out.

JUST BECAUSE YOU LEARNED A LOT
FROM YOUR LAST LOVER'S LEAP,

DON'T MEAN YOU AIN'T JUMPIN'
OFF A DIFFERENT CLIFF THIS TIME.

ATTENTION
WITHOUT
INTENTION IS
FLIRTATION.

When you go fishing
for compliments,
make sure you're
using the right bait.

A habit is either a blessing or a curse. Think about that when you find you've fallen into one.

NO MATTER HOW MUCH YOU TRUST YOUR HORSE, YOU'D BE FOOLISH NOT TO HITCH 'IM IN TOWN.

IT'S BETTER TO BE A WIDOWER'S SECOND WIFE

SECOND WIFE

THAN HIS FIRST.

IF YOU WANT A LITTLE EXTRA ATTENTION, ASK YOUR HUSBAND IF YOU CAN BORROW HIS SIX-SHOOTER FOR THE NIGHT.

Try not to make a ring
around the finger feel akin to
a rope around the neck.

Do not shoot
at the horse;
shoot at the
jackass ridin' it.

A DAY WITHOUT A SHARED LAUGH IS A SORRY DAY.

WHEN YOU GO TO TOWN, GO TOGETHER.

YOU CAN'T DROWN YOUR SORROWS,

THEY KNOW HOW TO SWIM.

LIFE IS NOT BEARABLE
WITH THE OPPOSITE SEX,
UNTIL IT'S UNBEARABLE
WITHOUT 'EM.

When a cowboy
gives you the key
to his truck,

you know you're
close to winning the
key to his heart.

DON'T MEASURE EACH OTHER IN INCHES.

SOME THINGS DON'T NEED ALL THE THOUGHT PEOPLE GIVE 'EM.

LOVIN' SOMEBODY FOR ALL
THEY'RE WORTH AIN'T QUITE
THE SAME AS LOVIN' SOMEBODY
FOR ALL YOU'RE WORTH.

WHEN YOU GET WIND OF A TAIL, YOU'RE FOLLOWING TOO CLOSE.

A NAG IS A
DRAG ON ANY
LOVE AFFAIR.

Sheep don't associate with wolves—

and for a dang good reason.

The art of horse sitting and
the art of marriage are easily
acquired if you keep at 'em from
dawn to dusk, day in, day out.

CRYIN' ABOUT
A BAD PAST
IS A WASTE OF
GOOD TEARS.

ALWAYS TRY TO MAKE FOLKS
HAPPY, EVEN IF THAT MEANS
GOING OUT OF YOUR WAY TO
AVOID 'EM.

THE BEST WAY TO GET AROUND SOMEBODY IS TO HUG 'EM.

If you don't have a
good reason to do something,
then you've got a sure-enough
good reason not to do it.

It's a lot cheaper to borrow money than to marry for it.

$$$

WHEN YOU SEE A TURTLE SITTIN'
ON A FENCE POST, YOU MAY NOT
KNOW HOW IT GOT THERE, BUT
YOU CAN BE SURE IT HAD HELP

TO LOVE AND
WIN IS THE
BEST THING.

TO LOVE AND
LOSE IS THE
NEXT BEST.

If you wanna say
NO,
it's best to say
it right away.

LOOKS MAY LAST AND THEY MAY NOT, BUT LOVE AND COURAGE TEND TO STICK AROUND.

DON'T BURN DOWN YOUR HOUSE TO KILL A RAT.

TO BRING
SOMEBODY INTO
YOUR LIFE,

TAKE A STEP
INTO THEIRS.

41

A woman's intuition comes from payin' attention to what's goin' on around her.

AS YOU GET MORE EXPERIENCED
IN ROMANTIC MATTERS, YOU'LL
NOT ONLY KNOW MORE, YOU'LL
KNOW BETTER.

You can't keep
trouble from visitin',
but you don't have
to offer it a chair.

THE BEST WAY TO REACH THE HEIGHTS OF ROMANCE

IS TO STAY ON THE LEVEL.

There are two kinds of
people in this ol' world:
those who believe there are two kinds
of people, and those who know better.

COMPLAININ' ABOUT YOUR PARTNER TO OTHERS IS A **BAD HABIT** THAT WILL LEAD TO WORSE ONES.

47

NEW AND IMPROVED CAN'T BEAT TRIED AND TRUE.

IT'S GREAT TO RIDE TOGETHER,
WORK TOGETHER, AND COME
HOME EXHAUSTED TOGETHER
AT THE END OF THE DAY.

When kissin' a cowboy in the rain,
make sure you both fit under his hat.

IF YOU DON'T QUARREL ONCE IN A WHILE,

★ ★ ★

ONE OF YOU IS JUST DUMB.

A STONE STOPS ROLLING WHEN IT LANDS NEAR THE KIND OF MOSS IT'S BEEN LOOKIN' TO GATHER.

You'll make
better progress
if you get out of
your own way.

If a woman looks old, she is old;
if she looks young, she is young;

**IF SHE LOOKS BACK,
FOLLOW HER.**

BE WARY OF
♥ PUPPY LOVE. ♥

IT CAN LEAD TO
A DOG'S LIFE.

IT'S BEST NOT TO CHEW ON SOMETHIN' THAT'S EATIN' YOU.

A LESSON EVERY COWGIRL SHOULD
LEARN IS WHERE HER BUSINESS
ENDS AND SOMEONE ELSE'S STARTS.

No need to buckle
on chaps and spurs
just to drive the
milk cows in.

Love fills you with the strong

BREATH OF LIVIN'.

IT'S PRUDENT TO SPEND LESS TIME TRYIN' TO FIGURE OUT WHO'S RIGHT AND MORE TIME TRYIN' TO FIGURE OUT WHAT'S RIGHT.

**BE SURE
THE GOIN' UP
IS WORTH
THE COMIN'
DOWN.**

FOR BETTER OR FOR WORSE MEANS

FOR GOOD.

The ranch is work
from sun to sun,

but love's work
is never done.

People whose manners are
on the absent side
are probably missin' more
than just their manners.

BE QUICK TO MEND FENCES.

WHEN YOUR SWEETHEART WANTS A LONG TALK,

YOU'D BETTER BE WILLIN' FOR A LONG LISTEN.

IF YOU'VE DONE IT, IT AIN'T BRAGGIN'.

SOMETIMES WHAT YOU'RE LOOKIN' FORWARD TO IS EXACTLY WHAT YOU SHOULD BE WATCHIN' OUT FOR.

You have to take
ranch country for what it is,
**not what it
ought to be.**

$$$

The cost of love is
not as important
as the value.

BRAND WHAT NEEDS TO BE BRANDED.

In all the history of the world, there was
ONLY ONE INDISPENSABLE MAN
& ONE INDISPENSABLE
WOMAN.

A LOT OF THINGS THAT DON'T
LOOK GOOD IN THEIR RAW FORM
TURN OUT TO BE PRETTY GOOD
WHEN THEY'RE FINISHED.

The best way to cure a pain in the behind is to kiss 'em goodbye.

SHARE YOUR WISDOM,
NOT YOUR PREJUDICES.

IF YOU GOTTA GRAB AHOLD
OF YOUR MATE TO TELL 'EM
SOMETHING, BEST THING TO
DO IS GRAB AHOLD OF YOUR
TONGUE INSTEAD.

You don't have to wait for someone to bring you flowers—plant your own garden.

THE BEST WAY
FOR A WOMAN TO
LOOK TEN YEARS
YOUNGER IS TO
GET RID OF THE
OLD FART SHE
SLEEPS WITH.

If a man thinks that a woman who can dog steers, ride broncs, and rope the wind is too much for him,

HE'S PROBABLY RIGHT.

IF A HORSE MAKES A FEW GOOD MOVES ON HIS OWN, HE SHOULD BE REWARDED SO THAT HE WILL DEVELOP OTHERS.

WOMEN HAVE TO
BE IN THE MOOD.
MEN JUST HAVE TO
BE IN THE ROOM.

The time to dance is when the music's playin'.

A wagonload of nursin'
don't amount to a
spoonful of sweetheartin'.

DON'T HANG YOUR HAT ON SOMEONE ELSE'S PEG.

WHEN THE SKILLET'S SIZZLIN', SOMETHIN'S COOKIN'.

♥ ♥ ♥

THERE ARE MANY KINDS OF BANDITS, SO SIT ON YOUR WALLET AND HOLD ONTO YOUR HEART.

Never go to bed mad.
Stay up and
fight it out.

It's not what you say to a horse that gets its attention.

IT'S HOW YOU SAY IT.

It's tough to walk away
from somethin' you love,
but sometimes it's the only way.

IF YOU CAN'T
TEASE SOMEBODY,
THEY AIN'T
IN LOVE WITH YOU.

Anybody who thinks they know everything

HASN'T BEEN AROUND LONG 'NUFF TO KNOW ANYTHING.

A woman
wanted by men
but disliked by
women is nothin'
but trouble.

WHEN YOU'RE WORKIN' A HORSE OR
DEALIN' WITH A MAN,
TAKE IT SLOW, TAKE IT EASY, AND
DON'T RUSH 'EM.

IF YOUR MIND'S SET TO RIDE A BUCKIN' BRONC,

YOU'D BETTER BE PREPARED FOR THE BRUISES.

There's no need for a lot of talkin'
when two people understand each other.

Never go quietly;

ALWAYS RAISE
HELL ABOUT IT.

THE SECRET TO A LONG LIFE IS TO BE WILLIN' TO GROW OLDER.

MARRIAGE IS LIKE A FIDDLE:
THE STRINGS ARE THERE WHETHER
THE MUSIC'S PLAYING OR NOT.

Nobody's credit is better than their money.

$$$

IT'S A DEAD-END CANYON
TO DWELL ON A LOVE
THAT MIGHTA BEEN.

If you find some happiness
inside yourself,

you'll start findin' it in a
lot of other places too.

IF YOU DON'T
EXPECT MUCH,
YOU AIN'T GONNA
GET MUCH.

♥ ♥ ♥
**Most marital graves
are dug with a
lot of little digs.**

CRACK YOUR OWN WHIP.
DON'T LET ANYBODY ELSE DO IT
FOR YOU.

IT'S NO BIG DEAL
CLEANING HOUSE,
COOKING MEALS,
OR DOING LAUNDRY.

MORE MEN
OUGHTA TRY IT.

DON'T BE SURPRISED IF A VISION THE NIGHT BEFORE

IS A SIGHT IN THE MORNING.

DON'T FIND FAULT; FIND A REMEDY.

Once you know
where you're goin',
just climb in the
saddle and stay
on the trail 'til
you get there.

About half your troubles come
from wantin' your way.

The other half come from getting' it.

A GOOD WOMAN WON'T
TAKE A MAN'S GIFT
UNLESS SHE'LL TAKE THE
MAN AS WELL.

OPPORTUNITY MAY
KNOCK JUST ONCE,
BUT TEMPTATION
IS A FREQUENT
VISITOR.

REMEMBER, WHEN AN
ARGUMENT'S OVER, IT'S DONE.

YOU'D BE PLUM LOCO TO START
IT UP AGAIN.

The more inches
you give a man,
the more he
becomes a ruler.

When you're pickin' flowers,
everybody gets along.
When it's time to muck the stalls is
when you find out how true your love is.

A CLEAR CONSCIENCE
IS A RESTFUL PILLOW.

JUST BECAUSE YOU DON'T SEE
TEARS ON THE OUTSIDE,
DON'T MEAN IT AIN'T POURIN'
ON THE INSIDE.

A WEDDIN' RING SHOULD CUT OFF THE WEARER'S CIRCULATION.

Don't let your sweetheart's **OLD FLAME** burn you up.

If you build walls
around yourself,

don't be surprised
if it gets kinda
lonely in there.

Look after the one you love,
and the one you love
will look after you.

THERE'S NO FUTURE IN LIVIN' IN THE PAST.

High steppers give
BUMPY RIDES.

IF YOU GET ALL WRAPPED UP IN YOURSELF, YOU'LL FIND YOU MAKE A PRETTY SMALL PACKAGE.

LOVE FROM AFAR

♥ ♥ ♥

IS TOO FAR OFF TO
DO YOU ANY GOOD.

OIL ALL THE WHEELS ON YOUR WAGON, NOT JUST THE SQUEAKY ONE.

Treat the one you love the same
as you'd treat your horse.
No one likes to be rode
hard and put up wet.

ALLOW NO WAR PARTIES IN YOUR BED.

NEVER MAKE A PROMISE
WITHOUT SOME IDEA
OF HOW YOU'RE GONNA
KEEP IT.

Don't try so hard to make your man a good husband that you don't have time to be a good wife.

YOU GOTTA GET AHOLD OF YOURSELF
BEFORE YOU CAN GET A HOLD ON
A GOOD MARRIAGE.

THERE IS A CHARM ABOUT A MAN WHO IS WILD.

DON'T FALL FOR IT.

No matter how
much he loves you,

**SOMETIMES HE'D
JUST RATHER
HAVE AN INCH
OF RAIN THAN
ANYTHING ELSE
IN THE WORLD.**

LOVE

IS A FIRE
YOU CAN'T BUY
INSURANCE FOR.

LOVE

is just one fool thing

after another.

A woman who intends to lean on her husband for support better be sure he stands on solid ground.

IF SOMETHIN' HAPPENS TO YOUR PARDNER AND YOU DON'T KNOW THEIR BUSINESS, YOU'RE IN FOR A BIG SURPRISE AND A LONG RIDE.

Don't be afraid to ride a
horse of a different color.

SOMETIMES IT'S A
NICE CHANGE OF PACE.

Being a friend to somebody you'd rather be in love with is like being invited behind the barn to look at the stars and **JUST LOOKIN' AT THE STARS.**

If you wake up and
find yourself a success,
YOU AIN'T
BEEN ASLEEP.

MARRIAGES MADE IN HEAVEN ONLY WORK

♥ ♥ ♥

WHEN THEY GET DOWN TO EARTH.

EVEN IF IT TAKES MORE THAN ONE THROW TO LAND A STEER AND TIE HIM, HE'S STILL ROPED AND TIED.

Ridin' the
gossip train
is not
GROUP
THERAPY.

DON'T WASTE TIME ON SOMEBODY YOU CAN EASILY RUN THE WHOLE LENGTH OF.

NEVER SHOW
YOUR ROLL.

**DON'T GO PUTTIN'
UP A GATE TO
SOMEONE'S HEART
'TIL YOU'VE
GOT A CORRAL
AROUND IT.**

145

Whether a horse turns out
to be a good cow horse or
a poor one pretty much depends
on the intelligence of the handler.

Women don't make
fools out of men;

they just give 'em
the opportunity.

IT'S EASIER TO STAY WELL THAN TO GET WELL.

SAYIN' WHAT YOU PLEASE
ONLY AS LONG AS YOU
PLEASE SOMEBODY,

AIN'T SAYIN' WHAT YOU PLEASE.

NATURE TEACHES, SHE NEVER PREACHES.

IF YOU'RE GONNA LEAVE, leave while you're still lookin' good.

Love is like a soft mattress:

it's easy to fall into

♥♥♥

but not so easy
to get out of.

IF YOU'RE HAVIN' TROUBLE WITH A MUSTANG,

CHANGE THE BIT.

YOU CAN'T KNOW EVERYTHING, NEITHER CAN ANYBODY ELSE.

Dwellin' on a PAST LOVE doesn't leave much room for FUTURE ROMANCE.

MOST EVERYTHING YOU HEAR ABOUT COWBOYS IS TRUE. BUT THE IMPORTANT THING IS—THEY TAKE CARE OF THE COWS.

Horses always start,
they never run out of gas,
and they will not get you
greasy.

Charity is not a luxury to be
acquired along the way.

It must be nurtured from
the heart's beginning.

A BIG HEART
IS BETTER THAN
A BIG HOUSE.

A GOOD MIND MOVES
WITH THE
PASSAGE OF TIME.

THERE'S A BIG DIFFERENCE
BETWEEN A GOOD, SOUND REASON
FOR DOIN' SOMETHIN' AND A
REASON THAT JUST SOUNDS GOOD.

Folks who have no

VICES

have very few

VIRTUES.

A good man's smile
is worth a million
winks from a
bar hopper.

WHEN THERE'S A DROUGHT, EVERYBODY IS DRY. WHEN IT RAINS, EVERYBODY GETS WET.

MOTHER NATURE

MAKES NO DISTINCTIONS.

DON'T SHARE YOUR BLANKET

IF YOU DON'T INTEND TO SHARE YOUR HEART.

MOST HARD-BOILED PEOPLE
are half-baked.

You know you're in love when there are only two places in the world:

where he is and where he's not.

NEVER LET YOURSELF BE DRAWN
INTO A GAME WHERE YOU DON'T
KNOW THE RULES—

ALL THE RULES.

WHEN THE HORSE DIES, GET OFF.

PREMATURE ULTIMATUMS GENERALLY RESULT FROM IMMATURE CONSIDERATIONS.

Approach love like a bowl of chili:

THE HOTTER THE BETTER.

Never ask a man
the size of his
SPREAD.

A MAN CAN BUILD A HOUSE, BUT IT TAKES A WOMAN TO MAKE IT HOME.

IT'S NOT A MIRACLE IF YOU FIND
AN ORANGE UNDER AN APPLE TREE;

SOMETHING AIN'T RIGHT.

WILD OATS CAN LEAD TO A SAD HARVEST.

Runnin' from problems
is a sure way of
runnin' into problems.

WHEN ONE PULLS AND ONE BUCKS, YOU AIN'T GONNA GET NOWHERE.

TO WIN, ALL YOU GOTTA DO IS
**GET UP ONE MORE TIME
THAN YOU FALL.**

DON'T LET A FOOL KISS YOU, OR A KISS FOOL YOU.

Sometimes it's smart to ask a man's advice,

but takin' it is another matter.

Lust is like a prairie rose:

IT LASTS WHILE IT LASTS.

EVERYTHING IS
BETTER SHARED.

Love is a rocky trail
THAT PROMISES
A SCENIC RIDE.

SAYIN' WOMAN IS THE **WEAKER SEX** MAKES ABOUT AS MUCH SENSE AS SAYIN' MAN IS THE **STRONGER ONE.**

DON'T WASTE YOUR TIME LOVIN' SOMEBODY YOU CAN'T LAUGH WITH.

Don't let anybody's OPINION kill your belief in YOURSELF.

Don't wait to know somebody
better to kiss 'em.

KISS 'EM

and you'll know 'em better.

IF A MAN CAN'T MAKE YOU

MISERABLE,

HE CAN'T MAKE YOU

HAPPY.

IF YOU WANTA STAY SINGLE,

LOOK FOR A PERFECT MATE.

when you

DISAGREE,

try not to be

DISAGREEABLE

about it.

A MAN WHO WEARS TWO FACES UNDER ONE HAT IS NOT TO BE TRUSTED.

BEIN' ON A DIET DON'T MEAN YOU
CAN'T LOOK AT THE MENU.

JUST DON'T MAKE A SELECTION.

A lot of what
a man knows,
a woman
knows better.

DON'T GET INVOLVED
WITH ANYONE WHOSE
WISHBONE
IS STRONGER THAN THEIR
BACKBONE.

SPRING CALVING
HELPS YOU
FORGET A HARD
WINTER.

A promise made is a promise kept.

That's how it is on the cowgirl trail.

DON'T BE AFRAID TO GIVE UP
ON A GOOD IDEA
IF THE FACTS
DON'T BEAR IT OUT.

The ties of
marriage are
not slipknots.

BEFORE YOU GET SERIOUS WITH A COWBOY, MAKE SURE HE VALUES YOU MORE THAN HIS TRUCK.

Virtue is its own punishment.

FAULTS ARE
THICK
♥ ♥ ♥
WHEN LOVE
IS THIN.

WHENEVER YOU GO AWAY, ALWAYS COME BACK BEFORE THEY LEARN TO GET ON WITHOUT YOU.

**Man is straw;
woman is fire.
When the devil
blows, it's hell.**

DO NOT SQUANDER YOUR PITY OR YOUR STRENGTHS.

BAD HABITS ARE THE
BARBED WIRE OF ROMANCE.
THEY CAN WEAR
THE HIDE OFF IT.

A MAN WHO WEARS SPURS HAS
HIGH EXPECTATIONS.

A WOMAN WHO WEARS SPURS
HAS A MIND OF HER OWN.

Marry somebody with brains enough for two,

AND IF YOU'RE LUCKY YOU'LL COME OUT EVEN.

YOU CAN'T GET AHEAD
OF ANYBODY
YOU'RE TRYIN' TO
GET EVEN WITH.

When you start to feelin' sorry for yourself, remember that whoever has to live with you has a lot more to feel sorry about.

ONCE HER BROKEN HEART MENDS,

♥ ♥ ♥

A WOMAN USUALLY FEELS LIKE A NEW MAN.

Just because a man says it's so,

DON'T MEAN
IT IS.

A HARVEST TAKEN TOO EARLY WILL GIVE YOU A THIN CROP.

Keep plenty of good hay in the barn
and you'll find it's a fact that a smart
horse never forgets the way home.

When you fall into
somebody's arms,
you're fallin' into
their hands as well.

RIDE THE HIGH COUNTRY,
SEE THROUGH GOD'S EYES.

RIDE THE DESERT,
FEEL GOD'S STRENGTH.

RIDE THE PRAIRIES,
HEAR GOD'S VOICE.

IT MAY BE MORE
ROMANTIC TO BE
THE FIRST LOVE,

BUT IT'S BETTER
TO BE THE LAST.

YOU GOTTA WEAR
THE BOOT TO KNOW
WHERE IT PINCHES.

IF YOU'RE FIXIN' TO GET
YOURSELF A GOOD STALLION,

★ ★ ★

DON'T GO LOOKIN' IN THE
DONKEY CORRAL.

Never venture
onto thin ice with
a fancy skater.

Horse sense and
affairs of the heart
are an unusual pair.

LEARN TO TIE SOME USEFUL KNOTS.

WHEN A MAN AND A WOMAN FIRST
GET MARRIED, THEY TELL EACH
OTHER EVERYTHING. AFTER A WHILE,
THEY KNOW WITHOUT TELLIN'.

FOOLIN' A MAN AIN'T ALL THAT HARD. FINDING ONE THAT AIN'T A FOOL IS A LOT HARDER.

WHEN THERE ARE TWO ON A HORSE, ONE MUST RIDE BEHIND.

Avoid any food
that would gag
a buzzard.

Big problems will pull you together. It's the little things that'll tear you apart.

WHEN SOMEBODY COMMENCES
TO FLATTERIN' YOU, THERE'S
GENERALLY MORE UP THEIR SLEEVE
THAN JUST AN ARM.

Never use a knife
to cut a tender
connection.

FROM TIME
TO TIME, FIND
YOURSELF
A PLACE SO
PEACEFUL THAT
YOU CAN ENTER
THE QUIET.

EVEN A FOOL CAN BE RIGHT SOME OF THE TIME.

Given a choice between
show and tell,
silence is golden.

If you've got love
in your heart,

you've got spurs
in your sides.

A HORSE IS CONSIDERED
WELL TRAINED
WHEN HE IS CONVINCED
THAT HE WANTS TO DO
WHAT YOU WANT
HIM TO DO.

233

IF WOMEN ARE FOOLISH, IT'S BECAUSE THE GOOD LORD MADE 'EM A MATCH FOR MEN.

NEVER KISS
A FOOL

. . . MORE'N ONCE.

CONVINCING YOURSELF
THAT A BAD IDEA
IS A GOOD ONE
IS A BAD IDEA.

NEVER SPUR A WILLING HORSE.

LEISURE TO REPENT IS A LUXURY ILL AFFORDED.

WHEN YOU DON'T HAVE A THING
IN THE WORLD TO WORRY ABOUT,
YOU GO AND GET **MARRIED**, AND
SUDDENLY THE WORLD IS A
WORRISOME PLACE.

First edition
23   5 4 3

Published by
Gibbs Smith
P.O. Box 667
Layton, Utah 84041

Orders: 1.800.835.4993
www.gibbs-smith.com

Designed by Renee Bond
Printed and bound in China

Gibbs Smith books are printed on either recycled, 100 % post-consumer waste,
FSC-certified papers or on paper produced from sustainable PEFC-certified
forest/controlled wood source. Learn more at www.pefc.org.

Library of Congress Control Number: 2018951515
ISBN 978-1-4236-5170-3